# ACRES OF DIAMONDS

# ACRES OF DIAMONDS

## RUSSELL CONWELL

**WILDSIDE PRESS**

# ACRES OF DIAMONDS

I am astonished that so many people should care to hear this story over again. Indeed, this lecture has become a study in psychology; it often breaks all rules of oratory, departs from the precepts of rhetoric, and yet remains the most popular of any lecture I have delivered in the fifty-seven years of my public life. I have sometimes studied for a year upon a lecture and made careful research, and then presented the lecture just once—never delivered it again. I put too much work on it. But this had no work on it—thrown together perfectly at random, spoken offhand without any special preparation, and it succeeds when the thing we study, work over, adjust to a plan, is an entire failure.

The "Acres of Diamonds" which I have mentioned through so many years are to be found in this city, and you are to find them. Many have found them. And what man has done, man can do. I could not find anything better to illustrate my thought than a story I have told over and over again, and which is now found in books in nearly every library.

In 1870 we went down the Tigris River.[1] We hired a guide at Baghdad to show us Persepolis, Nineveh and Babylon, and the ancient countries of Assyria as far as the Arabian Gulf. He was well acquainted with the land, but he was one of those guides who love to entertain their patrons; he was like a barber that tells you many stories in order to keep your mind off the scratching and the scraping. He told me so many stories that I grew tired of his telling them and I refused to listen—looked away whenever he commenced; that made the guide quite angry.

I remember that toward evening he took his Turkish cap off his head and swung it around in the air. The gesture I did not understand and I did not dare look at him for fear I should become the victim of another story. But, although I am not a woman, I did look, and the instant I turned my eyes upon that worthy guide he was off again.

1    The Tigris River is one of the major rivers of the Middle East. It flows through Turkey, Syria, and Iraq, running roughly parallel to the Euphrates River

Said he, "I will tell you a story now which I reserve for my particular friends!" So then, counting myself a particular friend, I listened, and I have always been glad I did.

He said there once lived not far from the River Indus an ancient Persian by the name of Al Hafed. He said that Al Hafed owned a very large farm with orchards, grain fields and gardens. He was a contented and wealthy man—contented because he was wealthy, and wealthy because he was contented. One day there visited this old farmer one of those ancient Buddhist priests, and he sat down by Al Hafed's fire and told that old farmer how this world of ours was made.

He said that this world was once a mere bank of fog, which is scientifically true, and he said that the Almighty thrust his finger into the bank of fog and then began slowly to move his finger around and gradually to increase the speed of his finger until at last he whirled that bank of fog into a solid ball of fire, and it went rolling through the universe, burning its way through other cosmic banks of fog, until it condensed the moisture without, and fell in floods of rain upon the heated surface and cooled the outward crust. Then the internal flames burst through the cooling crust and threw up the mountains and made the hills and the valleys of this wonderful world of ours. If this internal melted mass burst out and cooled very quickly it became granite; that which cooled less quickly became silver; and less quickly, gold; and after gold diamonds were made. Said the old priest, "A diamond is a congealed drop of sunlight."

This is a scientific truth also. You all know that a diamond is pure carbon, actually deposited sunlight—and he said another thing I would not forget: he declared that a diamond is the last and highest of God's mineral creations, as a woman is the last and highest of God's animal creations. I suppose that is the reason why the two have such a liking for each other. And the old priest told Al Hafed that if he had a handful of diamonds he could purchase a whole country, and with a mine of diamonds he could place his children upon thrones through the influence of their great wealth.

Al Hafed heard all about diamonds and how much they were worth, and went to his bed that night a poor man—not that he had lost anything, but poor because he was discontented and discontented because he thought he was poor. He said: "I want a mine of diamonds!" So he lay awake all night, and early in the morning sought out the priest.

Now I know from experience that a priest when awakened early in the morning is cross. He awoke that priest out of his dreams and said to him, "Will you tell me where I can find diamonds?" The priest said, "Diamonds? What do you want with diamonds?"

"I want to be immensely rich," said Al Hafed, "but I don't know where to go."

"Well," said the priest, "if you will find a river that runs over white sand between high mountains, in those sands you will always see diamonds."

"Do you really believe that there is such a river?"

"Plenty of them, plenty of them; all you have to do is just go and find them, then you have them." Al Hafed said, "I will go." So he sold his farm, collected his money at interest, left his family in charge of a neighbor, and away he went in search of diamonds.

He began very properly, to my mind, at the Mountains of the Moon. Afterward, he went around into Palestine, then wandered on into Europe, and at last, when his money was all spent, and he was in rags, wretchedness and poverty, he stood on the shore of that bay in Barcelona, Spain, when a tidal wave came rolling in through the Pillars of Hercules and the poor, afflicted, suffering man could not resist the awful temptation to cast himself into that incoming tide, and he sank beneath its foaming crest, never to rise in this life again.

When that old guide had told me that very sad story, he stopped the camel I was riding and went back to fix the baggage on one of the other camels, and I remember thinking to myself, "Why did he reserve that for his particular friends?" There seemed to be no beginning, middle or end—nothing to it. That was the first story I ever heard told or read in which the hero was killed in the first chapter. I had but one chapter of that story and the hero was dead.

\* \* \* \*

When the guide came back and took up the halter of my camel again, he went right on with the same story. He said that Al Hafed's successor led his camel out into the garden to drink, and as that camel put its nose down into the clear water of the garden brook Al Hafed's successor noticed a curious flash of light from the sands of the shallow stream, and reaching in he pulled out a black stone having an eye of light that reflected all the colors of the rainbow, and he took that curious pebble into the house and left it on the mantel, then went on his way and forgot all about it.

A few days after that, this same old priest who told Al Hafed how diamonds were made, came in to visit his successor, when he saw that flash of light from the mantel. He rushed up and said, "Here is a diamond—here is a diamond! Has Al Hafed returned?"

"No, no; Al Hafed has not returned and that is not a diamond; that is nothing but a stone; we found it right out here in our garden."

"But I know a diamond when I see it," said he; "that is a diamond!"

Then together they rushed to the garden and stirred up the white sands with their fingers and found others more beautiful, more valuable diamonds than the first, and thus, said the guide to me, were discovered the diamond mines of Golconda,[2] the most magnificent diamond mines in all the history of mankind, exceeding the Kimberley in its value. The great Kohinoor diamond in England's crown jewels and the largest crown diamond on earth in Russia's crown jewels, which I had often hoped she would have to sell before they had peace with Japan, came from that mine, and when the old guide had called my attention to that wonderful discovery he took his Turkish cap off his head again and swung it around in the air to call my attention to the moral.

\* \* \* \*

Those Arab guides have a moral to each story, though the stories are not always moral. He said had Al Hafed remained at home and dug in his own cellar or in his own garden, instead of wretchedness, starvation, poverty and death—a strange land, he would have had "acres of diamonds"—for every acre, yes, every shovelful of that old farm afterward revealed the gems which since have decorated the crowns of monarchs. When he had given the moral to his story, I saw why he had reserved this story for his "particular friends." I didn't tell him I could see it; I was not going to tell that old Arab that I could see it. For it was that mean old Arab's way of going around such a thing, like a lawyer, and saying indirectly what he did not dare say directly, that there was a certain young man that day traveling down the Tigris River that might better be at home in America. I didn't tell him I could see it.

---

2    The diamond mines of Golconda were some of the most famous and productive diamond mines in the world during ancient and medieval times. They were located in the region around Golconda, near present-day Hyderabad in southern India.

I told him his story reminded me of one, and I told it to him quick. I told him about that man out in California, who, in 1847, owned a ranch out there. He read that gold had been discovered in Southern California, and he sold his ranch to Colonel Sutter and started off to hunt for gold. Colonel Sutter put a mill on the little stream in that farm and one day his little girl brought some wet sand from the raceway of the mill into the house and placed it before the fire to dry, and as that sand was falling through the little girl's fingers a visitor saw the first shining scales of real gold that were ever discovered in California; and the man who wanted the gold had sold his ranch and gone away, never to return.

I delivered this lecture two years ago in California, in the city that stands near that farm, and they told me that the mine is not exhausted yet, and that a one- third owner of that farm has been getting during these recent years twenty dollars of gold every fifteen minutes of his life, sleeping or waking. Why, you and I would enjoy an income like that!

But the best illustration that I have now of this thought was found here in Pennsylvania. There was a man living in Pennsylvania who owned a farm here and he did what I should do if I had a farm in Pennsylvania—he sold it. But before he sold it he concluded to secure employment collecting coal oil for his cousin in Canada. They first discovered coal oil there. So this farmer in Pennsylvania decided that he would apply for a position with his cousin in Canada. Now, you see, the farmer was not altogether a foolish man. He did not leave his farm until he had something else to do.

* * * *

Of all the simpletons the stars shine on there is none more foolish than a man who leaves one job before he has obtained another. And that has especial reference to gentlemen of my profession, and has no reference to a man seeking a divorce. So I say this old farmer did not leave one job until he had obtained another. He wrote to Canada, but his cousin replied that he could not engage him because he did not know anything about the oil business. "Well, then," said he, "I will understand it." So he set himself at the study of the whole subject. He began at the second day of the creation, he studied the subject from the primitive vegetation to the coal oil stage, until he knew all about it.

Then he wrote to his cousin and said, "Now I understand the oil business." And his cousin replied to him, "All right, then, come on."

That man, by the record of the country, sold his farm for eight hundred and thirty-three dollars—even money, "no cents." He had scarcely gone from that farm before the man who purchased it went out to arrange for watering the cattle and he found that the previous owner had arranged the matter very nicely. There is a stream running down the hillside there, and the previous owner had gone out and put a plank across that stream at an angle, extending across the brook and down edgewise a few inches under the surface of the water. The purpose of the plank across that brook was to throw over to the other bank a dreadful-looking scum through which the cattle would not put their noses to drink above the plank, although they would drink the water on one side below it.

Thus that man who had gone to Canada had been himself damming back for twenty-three years a flow of coal oil which the State Geologist of Pennsylvania declared officially, as early as 1870, was then worth to our state a hundred millions of dollars. The city of Titusville now stands on that farm and those Pleasantville wells flow on, and that farmer who had studied all about the formation of oil since the second day of God's creation clear down to the present time, sold that farm for $833, no cents—again I say, "no sense."

\* \* \* \*

But I need another illustration, and I found that in Massachusetts, and I am sorry I did, because that is my old state. This young man I mention went out of the state to study—went down to Yale College and studied mines and mining. They paid him fifteen dollars a week during his last year for training students who were behind their classes in mineralogy, out of hours, of course, while pursuing his own studies. But when he graduated they raised his pay from fifteen dollars to forty-five dollars and offered him a professorship.

Then he went straight home to his mother and said, "Mother, I won't work for forty-five dollars a week. What is forty-five dollars a week for a man with a brain like mine! Mother, let's go out to California and stake out gold claims and be immensely rich."

"Now," said his mother, "it is just as well to be happy as it is to be rich."

But as he was the only son he had his way—they always do; and they sold out in Massachusetts and went to Wisconsin, where he went into the employ of the Superior Copper Mining Company, and he was lost from sight in the employ of that company at fifteen dollars a week again. He was also to have an interest in any mines that he should discover for that company. But I do not believe that he has ever discovered a mine—I do not know anything about it, but I do not believe he has. I know he had scarcely gone from the old homestead before the farmer who had bought the homestead went out to dig potatoes, and he was bringing them in a large basket through the front gateway, the ends of the stone wall came so near together at the gate that the basket hugged very tight. So he set the basket on the ground and pulled, first on one side and then on the other side.

Our farms in Massachusetts are mostly stone walls, and the farmers have to be economical with their gateways in order to have someplace to put the stones. That basket hugged so tight there that as he was hauling it through, he noticed in the upper stone next the gate a block of native silver, eight inches square; and this professor of mines and mining and mineralogy, who would not work for forty-five dollars a week, when he sold that homestead in Massachusetts, sat right on that stone to make the bargain. He was brought up there; he had gone back and forth by that piece of silver, rubbed it with his sleeve, and it seemed to say, "Come now, now, now, here is a hundred thousand dollars. Why not take me?" But he would not take it. There was no silver in Newburyport; it was all away off—well, I don't know where; he didn't, but somewhere else—and he was a professor of mineralogy.

* * * *

I do not know of anything I would enjoy better than to take the whole time tonight telling of blunders like that I have heard professors make. Yet I wish I knew what that man is doing out there in Wisconsin. I can imagine him out there, as he sits by his fireside, and he is saying to his friends. "Do you know that man Conwell that lives in Philadelphia?"

"Oh, yes, I have heard of him."

"And do you know that man Jones that lives in that city?"

"Yes, I have heard of him." And then he begins to laugh and laugh and says to his friends, "They have done the same thing I did, precisely." And that spoils the whole joke, because you and I have done it.

Ninety out of every hundred people here have made that mistake this very day. I say you ought to be rich; you have no right to be poor. To live in Philadelphia and not be rich is a misfortune, and it is doubly a misfortune, because you could have been rich just as well as be poor. Philadelphia furnishes so many opportunities. You ought to be rich. But persons with certain religious prejudice will ask, "How can you spend your time advising the rising generation to give their time to getting money—dollars and cents—the commercial spirit?"

Yet I must say that you ought to spend time getting rich. You and I know there are some things more valuable than money; of course, we do. Ah, yes! By a heart made unspeakably sad by a grave on which the autumn leaves now fall, I know there are some things higher and grander and sublimer than money. Well does the man know, who has suffered, that there are some things sweeter and holier and more sacred than gold. Nevertheless, the man of common sense also knows that there is not any one of those things that is not greatly enhanced by the use of money. Money is power.

Love is the grandest thing on God's earth, but fortunate the lover who has plenty of money. Money is power: money has powers; and for a man to say, "I do not want money," is to say, "I do not wish to do any good to my fellowmen." It is absurd thus to talk. It is absurd to disconnect them. This is a wonderfully great life, and you ought to spend your time getting money, because of the power there is in money. And yet this religious prejudice is so great that some people think it is a great honor to be one of God's poor. I am looking in the faces of people who think just that way.

I heard a man once say in a prayer-meeting that he was thankful that he was one of God's poor, and then I silently wondered what his wife would say to that speech, as she took in washing to support the man while he sat and smoked on the veranda. I don't want to see any more of that kind of God's poor. Now, when a man could have been rich just as well, and he is now weak because he is poor, he has done some great wrong; he has been untruthful to himself; he has been unkind to his fellowmen. We ought to get rich if we can by honorable and Christian methods, and these are the only methods that sweep us quickly toward the goal of riches.

* * * *

I remember, not many years ago, a young theological student who came into my office and said to me that he thought it was his duty to come in and "labor with me." I asked him what had happened, and he said: "I feel it is my duty to come in and speak to you, sir, and say that the Holy Scriptures declare that money is the root of all evil." I asked him where he found that saying, and he said he found it in the Bible. I asked him whether he had made a new Bible, and he said, no, he had not gotten a new Bible, that it was in the old Bible. "Well," I said, "if it is in my Bible, I never saw it. Will you please get the textbook and let me see it?"

He left the room and soon came stalking in with his Bible open, with all the bigoted pride of the narrow sectarian, who founds his creed on some misinterpretation of Scripture, and he puts the Bible down on the table before me and fairly squealed into my ear, "There it is. You can read it for yourself."

I said to him, "Young man, you will learn, when you get a little older, that you cannot trust another denomination to read the Bible for you." I said, "Now, you belong to another denomination. Please read it to me, and remember that you are taught in a school where emphasis is exegesis." So he took the Bible and read it: "The love of money is the root of all evil." Then he had it right.

The Great Book has come back into the esteem and love of the people, and into the respect of the greatest minds of earth, and now you can quote it and rest your life and your death on it without more fear. So, when he quoted right from the Scriptures he quoted the truth. "The love of money is the root of all evil." Oh, that is it. It is the worship of the means instead of the end. Though you cannot reach the end without the means. When a man makes an idol of the money instead of the purposes for which it may be used, when he squeezes the dollar until the eagle squeals, then it is made the root of all evil. Think, if you only had the money, what you could do for your wife, your child, and for your home and your city. Think how soon you could endow the Temple College yonder if you only had the money and the disposition to give it; and yet, my friend, people say you and I should not spend the time getting rich. How inconsistent the whole thing is. We ought to be rich, because money has power.

I think the best thing for me to do is to illustrate this, for if I say you ought to get rich, I ought, at least, to suggest how it is done. We get a prejudice against rich men because of the lies that are told about them. The lies that are told about Mr. Rockefeller because he has two hundred million dollars—so many believe them; yet how false is the representation of that man to the world. How little we can tell what is true nowadays when newspapers try to sell their papers entirely on some sensation! The way they lie about the rich men is something terrible, and I do not know that there is anything to illustrate this better than what the newspapers now say about the city of Philadelphia.

\* \* \* \*

A young man came to me the other day and said, "If Mr. Rockefeller, as you think, is a good man, why is it that everybody says so much against him?" It is because he has gotten ahead of us; that is the whole of it—just gotten ahead of us. Why is it Mr. Carnegie is criticized so sharply by an envious world! Because he has gotten more than we have. If a man knows more than I know, don't I incline to criticize somewhat his learning? Let a man stand in a pulpit and preach to thousands, and if I have fifteen people in my church, and they're all asleep, don't I criticize him? We always do that to the man who gets ahead of us. Why, the man you are criticizing has one hundred millions, and you have fifty cents, and both of you have just what you are worth.

One of the richest men in this country came into my home and sat down in my parlor and said: "Did you see all those lies about my family in the papers?"

"Certainly I did; I knew they were lies when I saw them."

"Why do they lie about me the way they do?"

"Well," I said to him, "if you will give me your check for one hundred millions, I will take all the lies along with it."

"Well," said he, "I don't see any sense in their thus talking about my family and myself. Conwell, tell me frankly, what do you think the American people think of me?"

"Well," said I, "they think you are the blackest hearted villain that ever trod the soil!"

"But what can I do about it?" There is nothing he can do about it, and yet he is one of the sweetest Christian men I ever knew. If you get a hundred millions you will have the lies; you will be lied about, and you can judge your success in any line by the lies that are told about you. I say that you ought to be rich.

But there are ever coming to me young men who say, "I would like to go into business, but I cannot."

"Why not?"

"Because I have no capital to begin on." Capital, capital to begin on! What! young man! Living in Philadelphia and looking at this wealthy generation, all of whom began as poor boys, and you want capital to begin on? It is fortunate for you that you have no capital. I am glad you have no money. I pity a rich man's son. A rich man's son in these days of ours occupies a very difficult position. They are to be pitied. A rich man's son cannot know the very best things in human life. He cannot. The statistics of Massachusetts show us that not one out of seventeen rich men's sons ever die rich. They are raised in luxury, they die in poverty. Even if a rich man's son retains his father's money, even then he cannot know the best things of life.

A young man in our college yonder asked me to formulate for him what I thought was the happiest hour in a man's history, and I studied it long and came back convinced that the happiest hour that any man ever sees in any earthly matter is when a young man takes his bride over the threshold of the door, for the first time, of the house he himself has earned and built, when he turns to his bride and with an eloquence greater than any language of mine, he sayeth to his wife, "My loved one, I earned this home myself; I earned it all. It is all mine, and I divide it with thee." That is the grandest moment a human heart may ever see. But a rich man's son cannot know that. He goes into a finer mansion, it may be, but he is obliged to go through the house and say, "Mother gave me this, mother gave me that, my mother gave me that, my mother gave me that," until his wife wishes she had married his mother.

Oh, I pity a rich man's son. I do. Until he gets so far along in his dudeism[3] that he gets his arms up like that and can't get them down. Didn't you ever see any of them astray at Atlantic City? I saw one of these scarecrows once and I never tire thinking about it. I was at Niagara Falls lecturing, and after the lecture I went to the hotel, and when I went up to the desk there stood there a millionaire's son from New York. He was an indescribable specimen of anthropologic potency. He carried a gold-headed cane under his arm—more in its head than he had in his. I do not believe I could describe the young man if I should

---

3    An exaggerated concern with fashion, style, or urban sophistication — especially in men. The term "dude" itself originated in the late 19th century as slang for a man who was overly dressed or preoccupied with appearance, particularly an urban man trying to play at being fashionable or cultured.

try. But still I must say that he wore an eye-glass he could not see through; patent leather shoes he could not walk in, and pants he could not sit down in—dressed like a grasshopper!

Well, this human cricket came up to the clerk's desk just as I came in. He adjusted his unseeing eyeglass in this wise and lisped to the clerk, because it's "Hinglish, you know," to lisp: "Thir, thir, will you have the kindness to fuhnish me with thome papah and thome envelopehs!"

The clerk measured that man quick, and he pulled out a drawer and took some envelopes and paper and cast them across the counter and turned away to his books.

* * * *

You should have seen that specimen of humanity when the paper and envelopes came across the counter—he whose wants had always been anticipated by servants. He adjusted his unseeing eyeglass and he yelled after that clerk: "Come back here, thir, come right back here. Now, thir, will you order a thervant to take that papah and thothe envelopehs and carry them to yondah dethk."

Oh, the poor, miserable, contemptible American monkey! He couldn't carry paper and envelopes twenty feet. I suppose he could not get his arms down. I have no pity for such travesties of human nature. If you have no capital, I am glad of it. You don't need capital; you need common sense, not copper cents.

A. T. Stewart,[4] the great princely merchant of New York, the richest man in America in his time, was a poor boy; he had a dollar and a half and went into the mercantile business. But he lost eighty-seven and a half cents of his first dollar and a half because he bought some needles and thread and buttons to sell, which people didn't want.

* * * *

Are you poor? It is because you are not wanted and are left on your own hands. There was the great lesson. Apply it whichever way you will, it comes to every single person's life, young or old. He did not know what people needed, and consequently bought something they didn't want, and had the goods left on his hands a dead loss. A. T.

---

4    Alexander Turney Stewart (1803–1876) was an Irish-born American entrepreneur best known as one of the first and most successful department store magnates in the United States. He played a key role in shaping modern retail.

Stewart learned there the great lesson of his mercantile life and said "I will never buy anything more until I first learn what the people want; then I'll make the purchase." He went around to the doors and asked them what they did want, and when he found out what they wanted, he invested his sixty-two and a half cents and began to supply a "known demand." I care not what your profession or occupation in life may be; I care not whether you are a lawyer, a doctor, a housekeeper, teacher or whatever else, the principle is precisely the same. We must know what the world needs first and then invest ourselves to supply that need, and success is almost certain.

A. T. Stewart went on until he was worth forty millions. "Well," you will say, "a man can do that in New York, but cannot do it here in Philadelphia." The statistics very carefully gathered in New York in 1889 showed one hundred and seven millionaires in the city worth over ten millions apiece. It was remarkable and people think they must go there to get rich. Out of that one hundred and seven millionaires only seven of them made their money in New York, and the others moved to New York after their fortunes were made, and sixty- seven out of the remaining hundred made their fortunes in towns of less than six thousand people, and the richest man in the country at that time lived in a town of thirty-five hundred inhabitants, and always lived there and never moved away. It is not so much where you are as what you are. But at the same time if the largeness of the city comes into the problem, then remember it is the smaller city that furnishes the great opportunity to make the millions of money.

The best illustration that I can give is in reference to John Jacob Astor, who was a poor boy and who made all the money of the Astor family. He made more than his successors have ever earned, and yet he once held a mortgage on a millinery store in New York, and because the people could not make enough money to pay the interest and the rent, he foreclosed the mortgage and took possession of the store and went into partnership with the man who had failed. He kept the same stock, did not give them a dollar of capital, and he left them alone and he went out and sat down upon a bench in the park.

\* \* \* \*

Out there on that bench in the park he had the most important, and, to my mind, the pleasantest part of that partnership business. He was watching the ladies as they went by; and where is the man that wouldn't get rich at that business? But when John Jacob Astor[5] saw a lady pass, with her shoulders back and her head up, as if she did not care if the whole world looked on her, he studied her bonnet; and before that bonnet was out of sight he knew the shape of the frame and the color of the trimmings, the curl of the—something on a bonnet. Sometimes I try to describe a woman's bonnet, but it is of little use, for it would be out of style tomorrow night.

So John Jacob Astor went to the store and said: "Now, put in the show window just such a bonnet as I describe to you because," said he, "I have just seen a lady who likes just such a bonnet. Do not make up any more till I come back." And he went out again and sat on that bench in the park, and another lady of a different form and complexion passed him with a bonnet of different shape and color, of course. "Now," said he, "put such a bonnet as that in the show window."

He didn't fill his show window with hats and bonnets which drive people away and then sit in the back of the store and bawl because the people go somewhere else to trade. He didn't put a hat or bonnet in that show window the like of which he had not seen before it was made up.

**\* \* \* \***

In our city especially, there are great opportunities for manufacturing, and the time has come when the line is drawn very sharply between the stockholders of the factory and their employees. Now, friends, there has also come a discouraging gloom upon this country and the laboring men are beginning to feel that they are being held down by a crust over their heads through which they find it impossible to break, and the aristocratic money-owner himself is so far above that he will never descend to their assistance. That is the thought that is in the minds of our people. But, friends, never in the history of our country was there an opportunity so great for the poor man to get rich as there is now and in the city of Philadelphia. The very fact that they get discouraged is what prevents them from getting rich. That is all there is to it. The road is open, and let us keep it open between the poor and the rich.

---

5    John Jacob Astor (1763–1848) was a German-American businessman who became the first multi-millionaire in the United States. He built his fortune through fur trading, real estate, and investing.

I know that the labor unions have two great problems to contend with, and there is only one way to solve them. The labor unions are doing as much to prevent its solving as are capitalists today, and there are positively two sides to it. The labor union has two difficulties; the first one is that it began to make a labor scale for all classes on a par, and they scale down a man that can earn five dollars a day to two and a half a day, in order to level up to him an imbecile that cannot earn fifty cents a day. That is one of the most dangerous and discouraging things for the working man. He cannot get the results of his work if he do better work or higher work or work longer; that is a dangerous thing, and in order to get every laboring man free and every American equal to every other American, let the laboring man ask what he is worth and get it—not let any capitalist say to him: "You shall work for me for half of what you are worth"; nor let any labor organization say: "You shall work for the capitalist for half your worth."

Be a man, be independent, and then shall the laboring man find the roar ever open from poverty to wealth.

The other difficulty that the labor union has to consider, and this problem they have to solve themselves, is the kind of orators who come and talk to them about the oppressive rich. I can in my dreams recite the oration I have heard again and again under such circumstances. My life has been with the laboring man. I am a laboring man myself. I have often, in their assemblies, heard the speech of the man who has been invited to address the labor union. The man gets up before the assembled company of honest laboring men and he begins by saying: "Oh, ye honest, industrious laboring men, who have furnished all the capital of the world, who have built all the palaces and constructed all the railroads and covered the ocean with her steamships. Oh, you laboring men! You are nothing but slaves; you are ground down in the dust by the capitalist who is gloating over you as he enjoys his beautiful estates and as he has his banks filled with gold, and every dollar he owns is coined out of the heart's blood of the honest laboring man." Now, that is a lie, and you know it is a lie; and yet that is the kind of speech that they are hearing all the time, representing the capitalists as wicked and the laboring man so enslaved.

Why, how wrong it is! Let the man who loves his flag and believes in American principles endeavor with all his soul to bring the capitalists and the laboring man together until they stand side by side, and arm in arm, and work for the common good of humanity.

He is an enemy to his country who sets capital against labor or labor against capital.

**\* \* \* \***

Suppose I were to go down through this audience and ask you to introduce me to the great inventors who live here in Philadelphia. "The inventors of Philadelphia," you would say, "why, we don't have any in Philadelphia. It is too slow to invent anything." But you do have just as great inventors, and they are here in this audience, as ever invented a machine. But the probability is that the greatest inventor to benefit the world with his discovery is some person, perhaps some lady, who thinks she could not invent anything.

Did you ever study the history of invention and see how strange it was that the man who made the greatest discovery did it without any previous idea that he was an inventor? Who are the great inventors? They are persons with plain, straightforward common sense, who saw a need in the world and immediately applied themselves to supply that need. If you want to invent anything, don't try to find it in the wheels in your head nor the wheels in your machine, but first find out what the people need, and then apply yourself to that need, and this leads to invention on the part of people you would not dream of before. The great inventors are simply great men; the greater the man the more simple the man; and the more simple a machine, the more valuable it is.

Did you ever know a really great man? His ways are so simple, so common, so plain, that you think any one could do what he is doing. So it is with the great men the world over. If you know a really great man, a neighbor of yours, you can go right up to him and say, "How are you, Jim, good morning, Sam." Of course you can, for they are always so simple.

When I wrote the life of General Garfield,[6] one of his neighbors took me to his back door, and shouted, "Jim, Jim, Jim!" and very soon "Jim" came to the door and General Garfield let me in—one of the grandest men of our century. The great men of the world are ever so. I was down in Virginia and went up to an educational institution and was directed to a man who was setting out a tree. I approached him and said, "Do you think it would be possible for me to see General

---

6    General James A. Garfield (1831–1881), who was a Union general during the American Civil War and later became the 20th President of the United States.

Robert E. Lee,[7] the President of the University?" He said, "Sir, I am General Lee." Of course, when you meet such a man, so noble a man as that, you will find him a simple, plain man. Greatness is always just so modest and great inventions are simple.

I asked a class in school once who were the great inventors, and a little girl popped up and said, "Columbus." Well, now, she was not so far wrong. Columbus bought a farm and he carried on that farm just as I carried on my father's farm. He took a hoe and went out and sat down on a rock. But Columbus, as he sat upon that shore and looked out upon the ocean, noticed that the ships, as they sailed away, sank deeper into the sea the farther they went. And since that time some other "Spanish ships" have sunk into the sea. But as Columbus noticed that the tops of the masts dropped down out of sight, he said: "That is the way it is with this hoe handle; if you go around this hoe handle, the farther off you go the farther down you go. I can sail around to the East Indies." How plain it all was. How simple the mind—majestic like the simplicity of a mountain in its greatness. Who are the great inventors? They are ever the simple, plain, everyday people who see the need and set about to supply it.

I was once lecturing in North Carolina, and the cashier of the bank sat directly behind a lady who wore a very large hat. I said to that audience, "Your wealth is too near to you; you are looking right over it." He whispered to his friend, "Well, then, my wealth is in that hat." A little later, as he wrote me, I said, "Wherever there is a human need there is a greater fortune than a mine can furnish." He caught my thought, and he drew up his plan for a better hat pin than was in the hat before him and the pin is now being manufactured. He was offered fifty-two thousand dollars for his patent. That man made his fortune before he got out of that hall. This is the whole question: Do you see a need?"

* * * *

I remember well a man up in my native hills, a poor man, who for twenty years was helped by the town in his poverty, who owned a wide-spreading maple tree that covered the poor man's cottage like a benediction from on high. I remember that tree, for in the spring— there were some roguish boys around that neighborhood when I was young—in the spring of the year the man would put a bucket there and

---

7    General Robert E. Lee (1807–1870) was the leading general of the Confederate Army during the American Civil War.

the spouts to catch the maple sap, and I remember where that bucket was; and when I was young the boys were, oh, so mean, that they went to that tree before that man had gotten out of bed in the morning, and after he had gone to bed at night, and drank up that sweet sap, I could swear they did it.

He didn't make a great deal of maple sugar from that tree. But one day he made the sugar so white and crystalline that the visitor did not believe it was maple sugar; thought maple sugar must be red or black. He said to the old man: "Why don't you make it that way and sell it for confectionery?" The old man caught his thought and invented the "rock maple crystal," and before that patent expired he had ninety thousand dollars and had built a beautiful palace on the site of that tree. After forty years owning that tree he awoke to find it had fortunes of money indeed in it. And many of us are right by the tree that has a fortune for us, and we own it, possess it, do what we will with it, but we do not learn its value because we do not see the human need, and in these discoveries and inventions that is one of the most romantic things of life. I have received letters from all over the country and from England, where I have lectured, saying that they have discovered this and that, and one man out in Ohio took me through his great factories last spring, and said that they cost him $680,000, and, said he, "I was not worth a cent in the world when I heard your lecture 'Acres of Diamonds'; but I made up my mind to stop right here and make my fortune here, and here it is." He showed me through his unmortgaged possessions. And this is a continual experience now as I travel through the country, after these many years. I mention this incident, not to boast, but to show you that you can do the same if you will.

Who are the great inventors? I remember a good illustration in a man who used to live in East Brookfield, Mass. He was a shoemaker, and he was out of work and he sat around the house until his wife told him "to go out doors." And he did what every husband is compelled by law to do—he obeyed his wife. And he went out and sat down on an ash barrel in his back yard. Think of it! Stranded on an ash barrel and the enemy in possession of the house! As he sat on that ash barrel, he looked down into that little brook which ran through that back yard into the meadows, and he saw a little trout go flashing up the stream and hiding under the bank. I do not suppose he thought of Tennyson's[8] beautiful poem:

---

8    Alfred, Lord Tennyson (1809–1892) was one of the most famous and wide-

> *"Chatter, chatter as I flow,*
> *To join the brimming river,*
> *Men may come, and men may go,*
> *But I go on forever."*

But as this man looked into the brook, he leaped off that ash barrel and managed to catch the trout with his fingers, and sent it to Worcester. They wrote back that they would give a five-dollar bill for another such trout as that, not that it was worth that much, but they wished to help the poor man. So this shoemaker and his wife, now perfectly united, that five-dollar bill in prospect, went out to get another trout. They went up the stream to its source and down to the brimming river, but not another trout could they find in the whole stream; and so they came home disconsolate and went to the minister. The minister didn't know how trout grew, but he pointed the way. Said he, "Get Seth Green's book, and that will give you the information you want."

They did so, and found all about the culture of trout. They found that a trout lays thirty-six hundred eggs every year and every trout gains a quarter of a pound every year, so that in four years a little trout will furnish four tons *per annum* to sell to the market at fifty cents a pound. When they found that, they said they didn't believe any such story as that, but if they could get five dollars apiece they could make something. And right in that same back yard with the coal sifter up stream and window screen down the stream, they began the culture of trout. They afterward moved to the Hudson, and since then he has become the authority in the United States upon the raising of fish, and he has been next to the highest on the United States Fish Commission in Washington. My lesson is that man's wealth was out here in his back yard for twenty years, but he didn't see it until his wife drove him out with a mop stick.

* * * *

I remember meeting personally a poor carpenter of Hingham, Massachusetts, who was out of work and in poverty. His wife also drove him out of doors. He sat down on the shore and whittled a soaked shingle into a wooden chain. His children quarreled over it in the evening, and while he was whittling a second one, a neighbor came along

---

ly read British poets of the 19th century. He served as Poet Laureate of the United Kingdom from 1850 until his death in 1892, succeeding William Wordsworth. He was a favorite of Queen Victoria, who admired his work deeply.

and said, "Why don't you whittle toys if you can carve like that?" He said, "I don't know what to make!"

There is the whole thing. His neighbor said to him: "Why don't you ask your own children?"

Said he, "What is the use of doing that? My children are different from other people's children."

I used to see people like that when I taught school. The next morning when his boy came down the stairway, he said, "Sam, what do you want for a toy?"

"I want a wheelbarrow." When his little girl came down, he asked her what she wanted, and she said, "I want a little doll's wash-stand, a little doll's carriage, a little doll's umbrella," and went on with a whole lot of things that would have taken his lifetime to supply. He consulted his own children right there in his own house and began to whittle out toys to please them.

He began with his jack-knife and made those unpainted Hingham toys.[9] He is the richest man in the entire New England States, if Mr. Lawson is to be trusted in his statement concerning such things, and yet that man's fortune was made by consulting his own children in his own house. You don't need to go out of your own house to find out what to invent or what to make. I always talk too long on this subject. I would like to meet the great men who are here tonight. The great men! We don't have any great men in Philadelphia. Great men! You say that they all come from London, or San Francisco, or Rome, or Manayunk, or anywhere else but there—anywhere else but Philadelphia—and yet, in fact, there are just as great men in Philadelphia as in any city of its size. There are great men and women in this audience.

Great men, I have said, are very simple men. Just as many great men here as are to be found anywhere. The greatest error in judging great men is that we think that they always hold an office. The world knows nothing of its greatest men. Who are the great men of the world? The young man and young woman may well ask the question. It is not necessary that they should hold an office, and yet that is the popular idea. That is the idea we teach now in our high schools and common

9    "Hingham toys" now refers to handcrafted wooden toys made in Hingham, Massachusetts, during the 18th and 19th centuries. This town, known as "Bucket Town," was famous for producing wooden buckets and other wooden items. As the demand for woodenware declined, local artisans began making toys like miniature furniture, dollhouse items, and small boxes. These toys were often sold to tourists visiting the area.

schools, that the great men of the world are those who hold some high office, and unless we change that very soon and do away with that prejudice, we are going to change to an empire. There is no question about it. We must teach that men are great only on their intrinsic value, and not on the position they may incidentally happen to occupy. And yet, don't blame the young men saying that they are going to be great when they get into some official position.

**\* \* \* \***

I ask this audience again, who of you are going to be great? Says a young man: "I am going to be great."

"When are you going to be great?"

"When I am elected to some political office."

Won't you learn the lesson, young man; that it is *prima facie*[10] evidence of littleness to hold public office under our form of government? Think of it. This is a government of the people, and by the people, and for the people, and not for the officeholder, and if the people in this country rule as they always should rule, an officeholder is only the servant of the people, and the Bible says that "the servant cannot be greater than his master."

The Bible says that "he that is sent cannot be greater than he who sent him." In this country the people are the masters, and the officeholders can never be greater than the people; they should be honest servants of the people, but they are not our greatest men. Young man, remember that you never heard of a great man holding any political office in this country unless he took that office at an expense to himself. It is a loss to every great man to take a public office in our country. Bear this in mind, young man, that you cannot be made great by a political election.

**\* \* \* \***

Another young man says, "I am going to be a great man in Philadelphia some time."

"Is that so? When are you going to be great?"

"When there comes another war! When we get into difficulty with Mexico, or England, or Russia, or Japan, or with Spain again over

---

10    Prima facie is a Latin term that means "at first glance" or "on its face." In legal and everyday use, it refers to something that appears to be true based on the initial evidence, unless it's later proven false.

Cuba, or with New Jersey, I will march up to the cannon's mouth, and amid the glistening bayonets I will tear down their flag from its staff, and I will come home with stars on my shoulders, and hold every office in the gift of the government, and I will be great."

"No, you won't! No, you won't; that is no evidence of true greatness, young man."

But don't blame that young man for thinking that way; that is the way he is taught in the high school. That is the way history is taught in college. He is taught that the men who held the office did all the fighting.

I remember we had a Peace Jubilee here in Philadelphia soon after the Spanish War.[11] Perhaps some of these visitors think we should not have had it until now in Philadelphia, and as the great procession was going up Broad Street I was told that the tally-ho coach stopped right in front of my house, and on the coach was Hobson, and all the people threw up their hats and swung their handkerchiefs, and shouted "Hurrah for Hobson!" I would have yelled too, because he deserves much more of his country that he has ever received. But suppose I go into the high school tomorrow and ask, "Boys, who sunk the *Merrimac*?" If they answer me "Hobson," they tell me seven-eighths of a lie—seven- eighths of a lie, because there were eight men who sunk the *Merrimac*.[12] The other seven men, by virtue of their position, were continually exposed to the Spanish fire while Hobson, as an officer, might reasonably be behind the smoke-stack.

Why, my friends, in this intelligent audience gathered here tonight I do not believe I could find a single person that can name the other seven men who were with Hobson. Why do we teach history in that way? We ought to teach that however humble the station a man may occupy, if he does his full duty in his place, he is just as much entitled

11    The Philadelphia Peace Jubilee, held from October 25 to 27, 1898, was a grand celebration marking the end of the Spanish-American War. As the first major city to host such an event, Philadelphia drew national attention with its elaborate festivities.

12    During the Spanish-American War, Richmond P. Hobson (1870-1937) was given command of the collier USS *Merrimac*. He attempted to sink that ship in the port channel to bottle up the Spanish squadron. On June 3, off Santiago in June 1898 and under heavy fire which disabled the steering gear of the collier, Hobson did sink the *Merrimac*, but was unable to fully block the channel. Hobson, along with his six men, was captured by Admiral Cervara of the Spanish fleet. While a prisoner of war in Cuba, he became a hero in the American press for his bravery in volunteering for what the press said was a suicide mission.

to the American people's honor as is a king upon a throne. We do teach it as a mother did her little boy in New York when he said, "Mamma, what great building is that?"

"That is General Grant's tomb."

"Who was General Grant?"[13]

"He was the man who put down the rebellion."

Is that the way to teach history?

Do you think we would have gained a victory if it had depended on General Grant alone. Oh, no. Then why is there a tomb on the Hudson at all? Why, not simply because General Grant was personally a great man himself, but that tomb is there because he was a representative man and represented two hundred thousand men who went down to death for this nation and many of them as great as General Grant. That is why that beautiful tomb stands on the heights over the Hudson.

I remember an incident that will illustrate this, the only one that I can give tonight. I am ashamed of it, but I don't dare leave it out. I close my eyes now; I look back through the years to 1863; I can see my native town in the Berkshire Hills, I can see that cattle-show ground filled with people; I can see the church there and the town hall crowded, and hear bands playing, and see flags flying and handkerchiefs streaming—well do I recall at this moment that day.

\* \* \* \*

The people had turned out to receive a company of soldiers, and that company came marching up on the Common. They had served out one term in the Civil War and had reenlisted, and they were being received by their native townsmen. I was but a boy, but I was captain of that company, puffed out with pride on that day—why, a cambric needle would have burst me all to pieces.

As I marched on the Common at the head of my company, there was not a man more proud than I. We marched into the town hall and then they seated my soldiers down in the center of the house and I took my place down on the front seat, and then the town officers filed through the great throng of people, who stood close and packed in that little hall. They came up on the platform, formed a half circle around

---

13    Ulysses S. Grant was the commanding general of the Union Army during the American Civil War, leading the Union to victory over the Confederacy. He later served as the 18th President of the United States. Grant's military leadership during the Civil War is widely regarded as a key factor in the Union's success.

it, and the mayor of the town, the "chairman of the selectmen" in New England, took his seat in the middle of that half circle.

He was an old man, his hair was gray; he never held an office before in his life. He thought that an office was all he needed to be a truly great man, and when he came up he adjusted his powerful spectacles and glanced calmly around the audience with amazing dignity. Suddenly his eyes fell upon me, and then the good old man came right forward and invited me to come up on the stand with the town officers. Invited me up on the stand! No town officer ever took notice of me before I went to war. Now, I should not say that. One town officer was there who advised the teachers to "whale" me, but I mean no "honorable mention." So I was invited up on the stand with the town officers. I took my seat and let my sword fall on the floor, and folded my arms across my breast and waited to be received. Napoleon the Fifth![14] Pride goeth before destruction and a fall. When I had gotten my seat and all became silent through the hall, the chairman of the selectmen arose and came forward with great dignity to the table, and we all supposed he would introduce the Congregational minister, who was the only orator in the town, and who would give the oration to the returning soldiers.

But, friends, you should have seen the surprise that ran over that audience when they discovered that this old farmer was going to deliver that oration himself. He had never made a speech in his life before, but he fell into the same error that others have fallen into, he seemed to think that the office would make him an orator. So he had written out a speech and walked up and down the pasture until he had learned it by heart and frightened the cattle, and he brought that manuscript with him, and, taking it from his pocket, he spread it carefully upon the table. Then he adjusted his spectacles to be sure that he might see it, and walked far back on the platform and then stepped forward like this. He must have studied the subject much, for he assumed an elocutionary attitude; he rested heavily upon his left heel, slightly advanced the right foot, threw back his shoulders, opened the organs of speech, and advanced his right hand at an angle of forty-five.

As he stood in this elocutionary attitude this is just the way that speech went, this is it precisely. Some of my friends have asked me if I do not exaggerate it, but I could not exaggerate it. Impossible! This

---

14    Napoléon Charles Bonaparte, 5th Prince of Canino and Musignano was born in Rome as the son of Charles Lucien Bonaparte and his wife, Zénaïde Bonaparte.

is the way it went; although I am not here for the story but the lesson that is back of it:

"Fellow citizens." As soon as he heard his voice, his hand began to shake like that, his knees began to tremble, and then he shook all over. He coughed and choked and finally came around to look at his manuscript. Then he began again: "Fellow citizens: We—are—we are—we are—we are— We are very happy—we are very happy—we are very happy—to welcome back to their native town these soldiers who have fought and bled—and come back again to their native town. We are especially—we are especially—we are especially—we are especially pleased to see with us today this young hero (that meant me) this young hero who in imagination (friends, remember, he said 'imagination,' for if he had not said that, I would not be egotistical enough to refer to it)?—this young hero who, in imagination, we have seen leading his troops—leading—we have seen leading—we have seen leading his troops on to the deadly breach. We have seen his shining—his shining—we have seen his shining—we have seen his shining—his shining sword—flashing in the sunlight as he shouted to his troops, 'Come on!'"

\* \* \* \*

Oh dear, dear, dear, dear! How little that good, old man knew about war. If he had known anything about war, he ought to have known what any soldier in this audience knows is true, that it is next to a crime for an officer of infantry ever in time of danger to go ahead of his men. I, with my shining sword flashing in the sunlight, shouting to my troops: "Come on." I never did it. Do you suppose I would go ahead of my men to be shot in the front by the enemy and in the back by my own men? That is no place for an officer. The place for the officer is behind the private soldier in actual fighting.

How often, as a staff officer, I rode down the line when the rebel cry and yell was coming out of the woods, sweeping along over the fields, and shouted, "Officers to the rear! Officers to the rear!" and then every officer goes behind the line of battle, and the higher the officer rank, the farther behind he goes. Not because he is any the less brave, but because the laws of war require that to be done. If the general came up on the front line and were killed you would lose your battle anyhow, because he has the plan of the battle in his brain, and must be kept in comparative safety.

I, with my "shining sword flashing in the sunlight."[15] Ah! There sat in the hall that day men who had given that boy their last hardtack, who had carried him on their backs through deep rivers. But some were not there; they had gone down to death for their country. The speaker mentioned them, but they were but little noticed, and yet they had gone down to death for their country, gone down for a cause they believed was right and still believe was right, though I grant to the other side the same that I ask for myself. Yet these men who had actually died for their country were little noticed, and the hero of the hour was this boy.

Why was he the hero? Simply because that man fell into the same foolishness. This boy was an officer, and those were only private soldiers. I learned a lesson that I will never forget. Greatness consists not in holding some office; greatness really consists in doing some great deed with little means, in the accomplishment of vast purposes from the private ranks of life, that is true greatness.

He who can give to this people better streets, better homes, better schools, better churches, more religion, more of happiness, more of God, he that can be a blessing to the community in which he lives tonight will be great anywhere, but he who cannot be a blessing where he now lives will never be great anywhere on the face of God's earth. "We live in deeds, not years, in feeling, not in figures on a dial; in thoughts, not breaths; we should count time by heart throbs, in the cause of right." Bailey says: "He most lives who thinks most."

If you forget everything I have said to you, do not forget this, because it contains more in two lines than all I have said. Bailey[16] says: "He most lives who thinks most, who feels the noblest, and who acts the best."

---

15    The imagery of a "flashing" or "glittering" sword appears in various literary and religious contexts. In the Bible, Deuteronomy 32:41 states: "When I sharpen My flashing sword, and My hand grasps it in judgment, I will take vengeance on My adversaries and repay those who hate Me."

16    Philip James Bailey, a British poet.